PR
HE KNOW

MW00882514

Samer Bazlamit has built .... to the alienated, brings close the distant, and endears the estranged. He Knows Your Name is a daily devotional that will inspire the reader to love, know, and serve God more.

Brett Fuller
Pastor, Grace Covenant Church- gracecov.org
Chaplain, Washington Football Team

With encouragement, passion, and depth of insight— Samer Bazlamit has written a devotional that is sure to draw you closer to the Father. The purity and power of each page will open your eyes to a deeper dimension of God's love for you!

Stephen Law
Pastor, Grace Covenant Church Capitol Hill
Author-Be A Man: Your Journey to Becoming Whole

He knows our name. Always has. The revelation by which He continues to make His name known, accessible and manifest in every situation and circumstance of life transfers His very life into ours. Samer, throughout this 31 day journey, has brought a fresh and needed focus on the persons of Father, Son and Holy Spirit. Without the burden of excess words or yet another theological opinion or perspective, Samer daily gets to the point and in so doing points us to fellowship with the person of Christ. The application each day becomes a personal journal of this journey. My prayer, like that of the author and another author writing to a church long ago, is that the *God of our Lord Jesus Christ, the glorious Father, may give you the Spirit of wisdom and revelation, so that you may know him better* (Ephesians 1:17).

Jim Critcher
Senior Associate Pastor, Grace Covenant Church, Chantilly, VA

HE KNOWS YOUR NAME

A 31 DAY DEVOTIONAL

SAMER M. BAZLAMIT

XULON PRESS

Xulon Press
2301 Lucien Way #415
Maitland, FL 32751
407.339.4217
www.xulonpress.com

Paperback ISBN-13: 978-1-6628-2324-4
Ebook ISBN-13: 978-1-66-282-3251

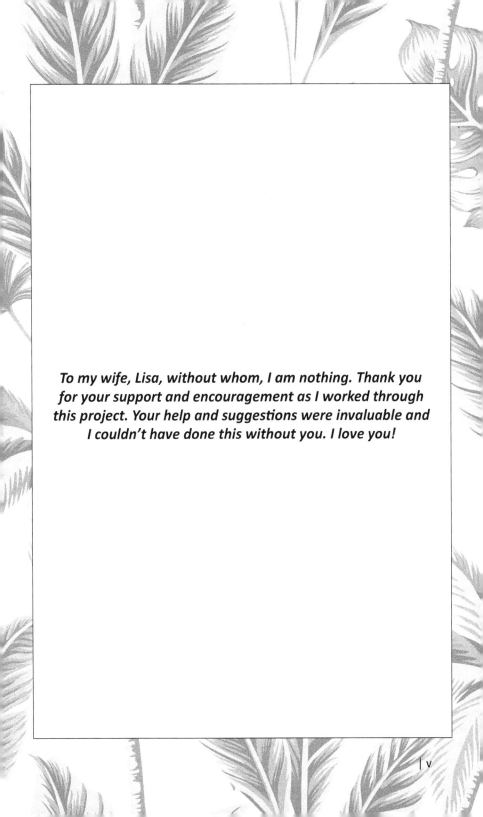

To my wife, Lisa, without whom, I am nothing. Thank you for your support and encouragement as I worked through this project. Your help and suggestions were invaluable and I couldn't have done this without you. I love you!

A VERY SPECIAL THANKS TO:

Pastor Jim Critcher for preaching the message that inspired this book. I'll never forget how the Lord spoke to me as you preached and the direction you gave me afterwards. That direction inspired this book, and I am forever grateful.

Pastor Danelle Perkins for her patience, encouragement, and coaching during the working of this project. Thank you for sticking with me as I poured out this labor of love!

This book would not be a reality if not for the two of you! I pray that God richly blesses you and your family for generations to come!

FOREWORD

S amer and I had the privilege of attending the same church before my move to South Carolina. Our Pastor (Brett Fuller) of Grace Covenant Church shared a true story about being invited to a professional football game by one of the players that attend our church.

The player invited our pastor and the pastor's son to visit him in the locker room immediately following the game. Accepting the invitation, they immediately made their way to the locker room after the game. A security guard who was stationed at the entrance of the locker room, immediately asked the purpose of their visit.

Our Pastor responded that he knew one of the players who invited them to visit him after the game. The security guard didn't believe him and would not allow them access to the locker room. Our Pastor then asked the security guard if he would be so kind to let the player know they were there, perhaps the player would come to see them. Reluctantly the security guard did so only to find out that our Pastor and his son were invited by the player and he allowed them to enter the locker room. What is the moral of this story? The permission to access the locker room wasn't in the fact that they knew the name of the player, it was in the fact that the player knew them and could call them by name. The book "He Knows My Name" you're about to read will give you a fresh and perhaps new perspective on the power of God knowing your name. He desires to have a personal relationship with each of us and when He calls our name, we experience His love and care. Samer is a true man of God who knows the power of God knowing his name. As you take this thirty-one-day journey, I pray you take advantage of all the tools that Samer has provided for you and that this wise step of reading this book will be a moment that will mark your walk with God.

Danell Perkins
Senior Pastor, Rise Community Church

KNOWING AND WAITING
(DAYS 1-2)

As you read through this devotional, you'll notice that I have broken the days down into various sections with multiple topics grouped together by days. I conclude each day with the "Application" potion: a prayer point, scripture reading, and provide space at the end of the book to journal as God speaks to your heart. I pray you utilize all of these to get the full value of that day's devotional.

The first topic covers days 1 and 2 is comprised of "knowing and waiting."

Oftentimes, we find ourselves waiting on God as we hope for Him to arrive in the midst of our situation and help us find a way out or provide an answer to our prayers. Even though we may feel like the answer never comes, we can take comfort in *knowing* that He knows our name, where we are in our walk with Him, what we need, and when we need it.

After reading these first two days, my prayer is that you will come to realize how much He knows who we are and will ponder how our stories might be different if we choose to wait on Him, even if it seems like an eternity. The Lord doesn't always show up when we want Him to, but He is always right on time.

Welcome. I pray that the next thirty-one days of reading and devotional time will be a tremendous blessing to you and help you grow in your walk with Christ.

Yours in Him,
Samer M. Bazlamit

DAY 1:

HE KNOWS YOUR NAME

How do you feel when you are called by your name? When you know someone knows your name and recognizes who you are, it's a great feeling, right? The feeling that you are known as an individual and someone of worth is very fulfilling.

Names are very important in the Bible. They represent history, significance, promise, and individuality. Of course, the greatest name of all is Jesus, the name of our Savior that brings power, salvation, freedom, and authority. While we should all strive to know His name in every sense of it, we can also take comfort in realizing that He knows our name. And He knows *your* name.

Let's take a look at Mary Madelene and how she reacted after the crucifixion of Christ to see how this thought played out in her life. Mary Magdalene went to the tomb of Jesus and found that He was not there. She told Peter and John, who came to see as well. They returned home but Mary stayed.

Notice what Jesus said to her in verse 15: He called her "woman," and Mary did not recognize Him. But then in verse 16, He called her "Mary," and she recognized her Savior.

You see, Jesus knows your name. He knows who you are and where you are! He will show up in times of sorrow just like He did for Mary, and when He does, He will call you by name. You will know it is Him. All you must do is respond!

John 20: 1-2 *Now on the first day of the week Mary Magdalene came to the tomb early, while it was still dark, and saw that the stone had been taken away from the tomb. ² So she ran and went to Simon Peter and the other disciple, the one whom Jesus loved, and said to them, "They have taken the Lord out of the tomb, and we do not know where they have laid him." (ESV)*

John 20: 11-16 *But Mary stood weeping outside the tomb, and as she wept she stooped to look into the tomb. ¹² And she saw two angels in white, sitting where the body of Jesus had lain, one at the head and one at the feet.¹³ They said to her, "Woman, why are you weeping?" She said to them, "They have taken away my Lord, and I do not know where they have laid him." ¹⁴ Having said this, she turned around and saw Jesus standing, but she did not know that it was Jesus. ¹⁵ Jesus said to her, "Woman, why are you weeping? Whom are you seeking?" Supposing him to be the gardener, she said to him, "Sir, if you have carried him away, tell me where you have laid him, and I will take him away." ¹⁶ Jesus said to her, "**Mary**." She turned and said to him in Aramaic,[b] "Rabboni!" (which means Teacher). (ESV)*

APPLICATION
Read:
John 10:27-28

Pray-That God will allow you to hear His voice and that you will know it is Him when He calls you. Ask God to quiet your mind so you can listen to His voice and respond when He calls you by name.

DAILY REFLECTION:
The Lord calls to all of us. In what ways has He called you? By name or another way?

DAY 2:

WAIT A LITTLE LONGER

I have a question for you. How does it make you feel when you want or need something and you are told to wait for it? Do you patiently say, "Okay," or do you become frustrated because waiting is so hard?

You see, we in the fallacy of our flesh are, by nature, impatient people. When we want something, we want it now! We like our fast food, microwaves, and our instant quick fixes. And while patience is a virtue, it's not one that we like to exhibit, especially when we consider what the Bible tells us about patience and how we must acquire it.

Waiting, however, can bring many benefits. The payoff is often sweeter when we have been forced to wait. We learn in our waiting that the effort needed to exhibit patience isn't so bad after all.

Then there is the concept of "delayed gratification." Wikipedia defines delayed gratification as: ***"the ability to resist the temptation for an immediate reward in order to receive a larger or more enduring reward later."***[1] If you learn to practice this principle, it will help you greatly in your walk with God as you learn to wait on Him.

Ever wonder what would have happened if Peter and John had waited at the tomb, how the narrative would have changed for them? They would have seen Jesus firsthand with Mary and experienced the miracle of His resurrection.

God is with us today, ever present in our time of trouble. When you are searching for Him but can't find the answer, do what Mary did: hold on and wait a little longer. Like Mary, you'll get your reward if you do for it was Mary alone who was given the privilege of announcing the resurrection of Jesus to the disciples!

John 20:6-11 *⁶ Then Simon Peter came, following him, and went into the tomb. He saw the linen cloths lying there, ⁷ and the face cloth, which had been on Jesus'[a]head, not lying with the linen cloths but folded up in a place by itself.⁸ Then the other disciple, who had reached the tomb first, also went in, and he saw and believed; ⁹ for as yet they did not understand the Scripture, that he must rise from the dead. ¹⁰ Then the disciples went back to their homes. ¹¹ But Mary stood weeping outside the tomb, and as she wept she stooped to look into the tomb. (ESV)*

John 20:17-18 *¹⁷ Jesus said to her, "Do not cling to me, for I have not yet ascended to the Father; but go to my brothers and say to them, 'I am ascending to my Father and your Father, to my God and your God.'" ¹⁸ Mary Magdalene went and announced to the disciples, "I have seen the Lord"—and that he had said these things to her. (ESV)*

APPLICATION
Read:
Lamentations 3:25
Psalms 27:14
Psalms 130:5-6
Psalms 37:34
Micah 7:7

Pray-That God will teach you to practice delayed gratification in every aspect of your life and that you will learn to wait on and for Him, even it means waiting a little longer than you would like. You just might find yourself with a great privilege from God, like Mary!

DAILY REFLECTION:
What makes it so hard for us to wait on God? After reading this devotional, do you see the benefits of waiting on Him? Why or why not?

UNDERSTANDING GOD'S WILL (DAYS 3-4)

I believe that one of the most important prayers you can pray is to seek God's will for your life. Understanding God's will should be the single most important goal of any Christian. It doesn't stop there, though. Once you know what God's will is for your life, you must do everything you can to make doing His will a priority.

We may not always want or like God's will, but when we choose to accept it, we can start to truly fulfil our calling. Our lives will then have real meaning as we set out to accomplish that which He has called us to do. Fulfilling God's will for our lives keeps us grounded and gives us sense of purpose as we strive for something greater than ourselves. That is our duty as Christians, to live beyond our own wants and needs as we seek to do His will for us on earth. Doing so will lead to true fulfillment and purpose above anything that we could accomplish in and of ourselves.

As you read and study the next two days, my prayer is that God will open your eyes to a place of understanding what He would have you do and that your obedience to that calling will lead to greater fulfillment and blessing in your life and the lives of those you touch.

DAY 3:

HIS WILL FOR YOUR LIFE

T he Bible calls David "a man after God own heart" (I Samuel 13:14, Acts 13:22). He battled Goliath for Israel, sang songs to God, wrote much of the Old Testament, and was anointed king of Israel.

But in this verse, we see that God's will superseded what David's will for his life was. David sought to build God's temple, which of itself was a good thing to accomplish. His motivation and will were in the right place, yet God said no. God's will for your life is always more important than your will for your life. Even if your will has the right motivation, God always sees the bigger picture.

In David's case, he was still able to participate in the temple project. He collected much of the material needed (1 Chronicles 22:14) and delegated Israel's leadership to help (1 Chronicles 22:17-19).

If you have breath in your body, then God is not finished with you. He has put dreams and visions inside of you, and He wants to see those birthed in your life!

1 Chronicles 22:7-11 *David said to Solomon, "My son, I had it in my heart to build a house to the name of the LORD my God. ⁸ But the word of the LORD came to me, saying, 'You have shed much blood and have waged great wars. You shall not build a house to my name, because you have shed so much blood before me on the earth. ⁹ Behold, a son shall be born to you who shall be a man of rest. I will give him* *rest from all his surrounding enemies. For his name shall be Solomon, and I will give peace and quiet to Israel in his days. ¹⁰ He shall build a house for my name. He shall be my son, and I will be his father, and I will establish his royal throne in Israel forever." (ESV)*

APPLICATION
Read:
Luke 22:42

Pray-That God will make your will for your life line up with His will for your life and that you will always put His will at the center of your being.

DAILY REFLECTION:
Why do you think it is so important to remain in the will of God?

DAY 4:

FINDING THE
CONTINUAL WILL OF GOD

D avid was the greatest king Israel ever had. He was victorious in war, a psalmist, and, as we know, a man whom God could trust.

But he was also a liar, a manipulator, a thief, an adulterer, a murderer, and a man of disobedience. David fell victim to those forces we all battle: the enemy and the flesh.

I often wonder why God didn't just take David after his many sins and disobedience. While I believe there are a number of reasons for that, like the fact that David held a special place in God's eyes or that he was quick to repent, the most important reason I believe is found in Acts 13:22.

It's the famous scripture we love to quote: "I have found David the son of Jesse a man after my heart." Can you quote the rest? "...who will do *all* my will." There it is. God knew David would accomplish everything He had for him to do, even though David did not know all that would entail.

God reminds us of this in Jeremiah 29 when He says: "I know," not "You know."

God had much for David to do, and He has much for you to do as well. God reveals His plans for our lives slowly and over time because He knows how much revelation we can handle.

What happened to David? The Bible tells us in 1 Chronicles 29:28 that he died at a good age, full of days, riches, and honor. His end was better than his beginning. Why not make that your story?

Jeremiah 29:10-11 *10 "For thus says the LORD: tWhen seventy years are completed for Babylon, uI will visit you, vand I will fulfill to you my promise vand bring you back to this place. 11 wFor I know the plans I have for you, declares the LORD, plans for welfare2 and not for evil, xto give you a future and a hope." (ESV)*

Application
Read:
Psalms 37:4
Matthew 25:23
John 14:14, 15:7

Pray- That God will reveal His continual will for your life as you obey the above verses and mature in Him.

Daily Reflection:
How would you go about finding the "continual" will of God in your life? What does that look like for you? Is finding His continual will for your life important ? Why or why not?

THE WILDERNESS EXPERIENCE (DAYS 5-7)

If you've lived for God for any amount of time, you have known the feeling of being alone in the wilderness. I have been there many times in my thirty-three year walk with God. One thing I have learned through my wilderness experiences is that my attitude during them makes all the difference in the world in how they turn out. I have learned not to curse my wilderness experiences but to count them for that they are: teachable moments from God where I can learn to wait on Him, listen to what He is saying to me, and grow from the experience. I realized that God is not done with me, and you need to realize this as well.

Going through the wilderness while living under the care of God is not a new phenomenon. Just ask the people for Israel, whom you will read about in the coming days. My prayer is that for the next three days, you will learn from these experiences and use them for a positive outcome in your own life so you can have a different attitude the next time you find yourself seemingly alone in the wilderness. Take heart—you are not alone. God is always there, and your wilderness just might be your way out.

DAY 5:

YOUR PERSPECTIVE IN THE WILDERNESS

I t has been said that how we look at our situations and circumstances will ultimately determine how we handle them. Our perspective has a lot to do with our reaction and attitude when we are in situations we don't like.

It doesn't take long to look into the Word of God to find great people who went through wilderness times. Job is one very evident example. He lost everything—his home, cattle, family, and even his health. But look at his perspective: "Though he slay me, yet will I trust him" (Job 13:15). His wife, on the other hand, told him to "curse God and die."(Job 2:9) Do you know what that tells me? Those around you may not always have the same perspective you do about your circumstances, even those who are closest to you.

Your perspective is entirely yours, and you would do you well to surround yourself with people who will give you a positive, encouraging perspective when times are tough.

When you're in the wilderness, you don't need anyone to tell you how bad your situation is; you need someone who will uplift you and strengthen you!

That's why the house of God is so important! You'll find strength, peace, and a word that will speak your situation and help you get through it. The world isn't going to help! Their perspective will tell you it's your fault. They aren't going to understand that

God has ordained this time in your life to bring the best out of you, just like Job's friends didn't see it that way.

Sometimes, like Job, when we have done nothing wrong, we still find yourselves in the wilderness. Nobody is exempt from these types of experiences. Remember that the Bible says the rain falls on the just and the unjust. (Matthew 5:45)

But remember your perspective! You are not alone! Either someone has been through what you're going through or someone after you will, and you can then be used by God to be an encouragement!

> **Job 1:20-22** *Then Job arose and tore his robe and shaved his head and fell on the ground and worshiped. ²¹ And he said, "Naked I came from my mother's womb, and naked shall I return. The LORD gave, and the LORD has taken away; blessed be the name of the LORD." ²² In all this Job did not sin or charge God with wrong. (ESV)*

APPLICATION
Read:
Luke 23:39-43
Job 42:12-17

Pray-That God will help you maintain the right perspective in difficult times, like the repentant thief on the cross. Pray that you will surround yourself with people who will encourage you in the house of God. God will turn your situation around, just like He did for Job.

DAILY REFLECTION:
Have you ever found yourself in a wilderness situation? How did that make you feel? What happened?

DAY 6:

HE IS WITH YOU
IN YOUR WILDERNESS

Deuteronomy chapter 1 ends with Moses recalling the defeat of the Israelites at the hand of the Amorites and how they wept before the Lord. We pick up in chapter 2. Let's look at what Israel did. First of all, they turned. Do you ever feel like God is taking you in a different direction that you thought you were going to go? God may take you down a straight path, but then there may be some turns here and there.

When you feel lost but are able to still trust God, then you will have a peace that will bring you through. God won't let you down!

Now look where they ended up. God took them into the wilderness. You see, God doesn't mess around. Sometimes you will head straight into your wilderness, and there's nothing you can do about it. That's because He wants you there! Moses wrote that they turned and journeyed into the wilderness "as the Lord spake." Moses was being obedient to the will of God!

If God leads you into the wilderness, He will lead you out! And He will be with you in your wilderness because He wants to work the problems, struggles, and shortcomings out of your life.

The Israelites now found themselves right in front of a mountain, not a good place to be. The Bible says they were there many days.

But now comes my favorite part. In verse 3, God said: "You have compassed this mountain long enough...turn you northward."

You see, God knows just how much trouble you can handle, and He knows just when to say you've had enough. He told Moses to turn north. In other words, it's time to go up. You won't always be down—God will take you up!

Whatever your mountain might be, whether a struggle, problem, situation, or temptation, God will bring you out!

Deuteronomy 2:1-2 *"Then we turned and journeyed into the wilderness in the direction of the Red Sea, ᵉas the* LORD *told me. And for many days we traveled around Mount Seir. ² Then the* LORD *said to me, ³ 'You have been traveling around this mountain country ᶠlong enough. Turn northward. (ESV)*

APPLICATION
Read:
Deuteronomy 2:7

Pray-That you will still seek God and trust Him in your wilderness and rest in knowing that He is always there!

DAILY REFLECTION:
If you have ever found yourself in the wilderness, did you realize that God was with you the entire time? Why or why not? How did that affect your faith in Him?

DAY 7:

YOUR WILDERNESS
IS YOUR WAY OUT

We know from Genesis chapter 35:23-26 that Jacob had twelve sons. We also know that Joseph was Jacob's favorite, according to Genesis 37:3, and showed his extra love by making him a coat of many colors.

This made Joseph's brothers jealous of him. Then he had a few dreams, and we see him telling his brothers that they were going to bow down before him. Well, that really made them mad, so they conspired against him and threw him into a pit.

Now Joseph didn't ask for these dreams. God gave them to him. But his brothers did not like them and thus thrust Joseph into the pit, beginning the start of his own wilderness experience. Sometimes things happen to that you don't ask for, but remember, there's always a purpose behind it.

Then we read later in Genesis 37 that his brothers pulled him out of the pit and sold him into slavery. Joseph had now gone from the frying pan into the fire. Joseph was sold to the Ishmaelites and then sent to Egypt. And thus, we have the beginning of God's people, the Jews, ending up in Egypt with their deliverance ultimately coming from Joseph's wilderness.

As we read, remember that when you're all alone or find yourself locked up in a prison of life, God will be with you!

Jacob and his sons ended up experiencing a famine and saw that there was food in Egypt. Jacob sent his sons to Egypt, and when they saw Joseph, who had not become governor over the land, they didn't recognize him. He fed them while keeping his identity secret.

But now we see that everything Joseph went through was ultimately to the saving of Israel and his sons. When they all went down to Egypt and dwelled there, Joseph revealed himself to his father and brethren.

God used everything that happened to Joseph as a means of saving Jacob. His wilderness became a way out for others. And Joseph realized this.

Joseph went through his wilderness and helped deliver his entire family, and one day, all of Israel would find deliverance from Egypt. Your wilderness is your way out.

Genesis 39:21-23 *The LORD was with Joseph, and he became a successful man, and he was in the house of his Egyptian master. But the LORD was with Joseph and showed him steadfast love and gave him favor in the sight of the keeper of the prison. ²² And the keeper of the prison put Joseph in charge of all the prisoners who were in the prison. Whatever was done there, he was the one who did it. ²³ The keeper of the prison paid no attention to anything that was in Joseph's charge, because the LORD was with him. And whatever he did, the LORD made it succeed. (ESV)*

APPLICATION
Read:
Genesis 45:4-7
Genesis 50:18-21

Pray-That God will help you understand your purpose in your wilderness and who might gain deliverance and freedom from your own wilderness experience.

DAILY REFLECTION:
How has this section on the wilderness changed how you view these times in your life?

THE ONE THING
(DAYS 8-10)

We know that God is omnipotent (all-powerful), omniscient (all-knowing), and omnipresent (everywhere at once). So how in the world could I write a devotional about the one thing He can't do, the one thing He doesn't know, and the one thing He won't remember?

You'll have to read on to find out! And in doing so, I hope you will have a fresh take on just how awesome this God of the universe we serve is!

I remember when I preached this message the reaction that I got. This is a different yet very powerful take on who we call "Father." I hope you find it to be true for you when you read it as well. What a mighty God we serve!

DAY 8:

THE ONE THING
GOD DOESN'T KNOW

I f there is one thing that God loves, it is our worship and our praise. He loves it when His people express their love, appreciation, and honor to Him. In fact, we were created to worship Him. The reason God loves our praise and worship is because it is the only way we can give something back to Him, and it comes from our own effort and freewill. God loves our praise so much that He inhabits, or dwells, in it. You see, when you begin to praise God, He says, "Wait a minute! My people are praising Me, and I've got to see what is going on and visit them."

God loves the worship and praise of His people, and He doesn't want to share His worship with anybody else. For it was He alone who created us and He alone who bore our sins upon the cross. For this reason, He makes it clear from the beginning that He is the only God who exists.

The fact that the Egyptians held God's people in bondage for all those years was not the only reason they were God's enemy. It was the main reason, but not the only one.

The Egyptians were idolaters, and God gave His people specific instructions to not follow in their footsteps. God commanded His people not to worship idols like Egypt and other nations (Deuteronomy 7:17-18, 22, 24-25).

God promised to protect His people but made it clear that they were to have no other gods.

Buddhists also serve many gods—manmade metal gods, I might add. Muslims serve Allah.

And while I can appreciate these people's unwavering devotion to their gods, I have just one problem with that. None of these gods died for me. None of these gods shed perfect blood for me. And certainly, none of these gods ever rose from the grave for me!

In Greek mythology, their gods often ridiculed and mocked men. They punished men and made life on earth miserable.

Why would anybody want to serve a god like that? So, what's the one thing God doesn't know? Read below in the application to find out!

I'm thankful that I know the one true God. Aren't you?

Deuteronomy 6:4 *Hear, O Israel: ᵈThe LORD our God, the LORD is one. (ESV)*

Application
Read:
Isaiah 44:8

Pray-That you will grow in your relationship with God and repent over any idols that you worship. Pray that God will take His rightful place in your heart and in your life.

Daily Reflection:
When you read about God not knowing any other god, does that change how you view Him in all His majesty? Why or why not?

DAY 9:

THE ONE THING
GOD CAN'T DO

I am convinced that if we could learn to just simply take God at His Word, our lives would become so much simpler. Why? The whole basis for faith comes from our belief in the Word of God. We believe what the Bible says, and we stand on its promises. That's faith.

God will respond to your faith, and what you believe will come to pass when it is according to His Word.

God can't lie because the Bible tells us that He is the Word. So, when He speaks, it is He Himself that is being manifested, and it is truth.

You know the thing about children? They'll believe anything you tell them. They don't have the mental capacity or reasoning to question what you say.

So, when Jesus said, "Whosoever shall not receive the Kingdom of God as a little child shall in no wise enter in," (Mark 10:15, Luke 18;17) that is exactly what He meant.

Don't question God; just believe what He says! That scripture appears twice in the Bible in both Mark and Luke, which tells me there is some emphasis to it. Just take God at His Word, receiving it like a child receives what you tell them—with no doubt whatsoever.

John 14:6 *Jesus said to him, "I am the way, and the truth, and the life. No one comes to the Father except through me." (ESV)*

Application
Read:
John 1:1,14

Pray-That you will exercise your faith and take Him at His Word and that you will learn to trust Him like a child trusts a parent for He is our faithful Father.

Daily Reflection:
How does it make you feel to know that when God speaks to you personally, through His Word or otherwise, He can only speak the truth?

DAY 10:

THE ONE THING GOD WON'T REMEMBER

We know that we serve a God who is omniscient. That is, He knows everything. The Bible makes it clear in many passages with scriptures like this: "I declare the end from the beginning" (Isa. 46:10) and "Nothing in all creation is hidden from God's sight" (Heb. 4:13).

God knows all and sees all. And He knows that we are sinners, created in His image yet subject to the fallen nature of Adam. But with His blood, He purchased our salvation and provided a way of escape from the wages of our sin, which is death.

I am also thankful that God even goes beyond that. He gives us a beautiful picture of what He does for us in His redemptive work—He remembers our sins know more. I like how He says in our opening verse that He removes our transgressions from us as far as the east is from the west. In other words, our transgressions are moved far away from us! Notice that this verse is continual. It shows ongoing action and is not limited to a onetime event. That means His blood still has the redemptive the power it had on Calvary. And even if we still sin, when we repent, He removes that sin from us.

Not that His grace gives us a license to sin—God forbid, as Paul says (Romans 6:15). And the best part? He remembers our sins know more. (Hebrews 8:12) I'm glad there is one thing that God won't remember! Aren't you?

Psalms 103:12 *As far as the east is from the west, so far does he remove our transgressions from us.* *(ESV)*

APPLICATION
Read:
Hebrews 8:10-12
1 John 1:9

Pray-With thanksgiving to God for the redemptive power of His blood and that you will always be quick to repent. Pray that you will live an obedient life pleasing to Him, one that is free from sin in the best way that you can.

DAILY REFLECTION:
How wonderful is it and how thankful does it make you to know that God will no longer remember your sins when you repent and turn to Him?

THE WEAPONS AND
ARMOR OF OUR WARFARE
(DAYS 11-20)

This next section of our devotional is quite lengthy and covers many topics that deal with spiritual warfare. You see, while we can enjoy the blessings and protection of grace from God, we must also realize that there is an enemy who would more than like to see our destruction.

Whether we want to admit it or not, we are in a spiritual war. Our enemy wants to defeat us at all cost, but God has given us tools to attack and defend: our weapons and our armor. We will dig deep over the next ten days into these weapons and armor through the lens of Scripture—what they are and how to use them. My hope is that after this section, you will be a much more effective warrior in God's kingdom and be able to utilize what He has given you for those times you face the enemy. In doing so, you can help move God's kingdom forward. You are more than a conqueror!

DAY 11:

ARE YOU AFFLICTED?

I love Isaiah because he wrote so many beautiful passages that depict Christ. Isaiah is known as the greatest Old Testament prophet. He was the prophet of redemption, and his book portrays our Lord's birth and promises.

I also enjoy how Isaiah wrote that God led him too and leads those who are afflicted. Maybe, friend, you are in a storm right now and tossed with a tempest. God will give you a sure foundation, a beautiful foundation, and set your feet upon a rock.

We have a promise from God that when we are afflicted, He will be our solid foundation. His Word also tells us how to handle affliction.

James told us, "Is any of you afflicted, let him pray "(James 5:13). Prayer is a powerful weapon, our direct access to God and so critical for our victory.

After that beautiful list of spiritual armor Paul told us to put on, he appealed to us in Ephesians 6:18, "Praying always with all prayer and supplication in the Spirit."

If we are afflicted, we must pray and put on the whole armor of God. Prayer is how we access the power of the Spirit to overcome the enemy.

Isaiah 54 tells us that we are taught of God. After standing on His foundation, our children will have peace. You see, God cares and loves our children deeply and will protect them when we are obedient and set on the Rock.

Isaiah 54:14 tells us the key and lets us know what will keep us—we must be established in this righteousness, or right standing with God our Father.

When we are in a place of right standing, living rightly and obedient to God, we have tremendous promises from Him. As you read below in Isaiah, notice what righteousness will do for you. It will keep oppression from you, and terror will not come near you.

> **Isaiah 54:11-15** *"O afflicted one, storm-tossed and not comforted, behold, I will set your stones in antimony, and lay your foundations with sapphires. [12] I will make your pinnacles of agate, your gates of carbuncles, and all your wall of precious stones. [13] All your children shall be taught by the LORD, and great shall be the peace of your children. [14] In righteousness you shall be established; you shall be far from oppression, for you shall not fear; and from terror, for it shall not come near you. [15] If anyone stirs up strife, it is not from me; whoever stirs up strife with you shall fall because of you." (ESV)*

APPLICATION
Read:
James 5:13

Pray-That when you feel afflicted, God will cover you with His peace and that you will be able to put on the whole armor of God.

DAILY REFLECTION:
Think back to a time when you went through affliction. How did God see you through? How does that help you prepare for the next time you are afflicted?

DAY 12:

FEAR NOT

F ear is the weapon of terror. It will paralyze you and keep you from fulfilling the purposes of God in your life. But the Bible says you shall fear not and that when God establishes you in righteousness, terror will not come near you. Praise God!

As I started this study, I found similarities between Isaiah 54 and Ephesians 6. In Isaiah, it says righteousness will keep terror from us, and in Ephesians, it says the breastplate of righteousness protects us—our body armor, if you will.

When we are in right standing with God, we are in a very powerful place that will keep us and protect us from the enemy.

Isaiah tells us in verse 15 that surely our enemies will gather against us. We do have enemies, those who don't like what we do or stand for. The devil will use those to hinder us, but our God says they shall fall.

I like that God says our enemies shall fall. Just like Jesus said when He told Peter, "Upon this rock I will build my church and the gates of hell shall not prevail against it." (Matthew 16:18)

You see, we are a part of God's church. He will protect His church that He loves and died for. No matter what is thrown your way, God said that it shall not prevail.

All you need to do is make sure you are in right standing with God. Amen?

Isaiah 54:14-15: *In righteousness shalt thou be established: thou shalt be far from oppression; for thou shalt not fear: and from terror; for it shall not come near thee. ¹⁵Behold, they shall surely gather together, but not by me: whosoever shall gather together against thee shall fall for thy sake. (KJV)*

APPLICATION
Read:
Matthew 16:18

Pray-That God will protect you against your enemies and that He will establish your feet upon solid ground. Pray that you are in right standing with God so that His grace and mercy will cover you.

DAILY REFLECTION:
When you think about the word "fear," what emotions come to mind? Does what God say in His Word about fear change your perspective? Why or why not?

DAY 13:

NO WEAPON

I saiah continues to show us just how powerful God is and just how much sovereignty He wields. Let's start with Isaiah 54:16: "Behold, I have created the smith that bloweth the coals in the fire. I have created the waster to destroy." We know who the waster is. Jesus told us in John 10:10, "The thief cometh but to steal, kill and destroy."

But when we begin to understand that it was God who created the waster, the enemy, in the first place, we realize just how in control God is. The enemy can only do to you what God allows.

The devil is not in control. No matter how much hell is in your life, no matter how bleak things may look, no matter how hopeless your situation may seem, the enemy is not in control. Our God is, completely.

God has always and will always be in control of everything!

He is the Lord who created the smith where the weapons are forged and the waster to destroy. He turns up the fire to purge us, to make us better! Let's keep the proper prospective. God created the waster and will destroy him.

No weapon that is formed against you shall prosper!

No fiery darts, no lies, no sickness, no false accusers—no weapon that is formed!

Praise God!

God doesn't stop there. He goes on to say in His Word that every tongue that rises against you in judgement (gossip, lies, false accusations) He will condemn because of our heritage in Christ and your right standing in Him.

> **Isaiah 54:17** *No weapon that is formed against thee shall prosper; and every tongue that shall rise against thee in judgment thou shalt condemn. This is the heritage of the servants of the LORD, and their righteousness is of me, saith the LORD. (ESV)*

APPLICATION
Read:
Ephesians 6:10-18

Pray-That you will learn to put on the whole armor of God on a daily basis and be able to stand at the time of the attack of the enemy, being protected by God's spiritual armor.

DAILY REFLECTION:
How does it make you feel to know that God's Word says no weapon formed against you shall prosper?

DAY 14:
YOUR VICTORY IN CHRIST

J ust as our military has an incredible arsenal of weapons, God's army has a vast array of spiritual weapons. Use them! Start with prayer. This powerful weapon can change any situation.

Feeling tempted or attacked? Pull out the sword of the Spirit and start quoting the Word for it is quick, powerful, and sharper than any two-edged sword. It will send the enemy running in fear.

Guard your mind! Protect your thoughts! When you win the battle in your mind, you've won the battle over your entire life. It starts with our thinking.

I know this isn't deep today, but please listen closely. I want you to understand that if you stay covered and protected, you will have the victory that you are seeking.

Maybe you are in a battle right now and see those around you being blessed. You are struggling to stay positive and keep the faith while the enemy tosses problem after problem your way. Let me remind you that you are not defeated, you are not alone, and you are more than a conquer. Remember God's promises!

What did God tell King Jehoshaphat when he went to fight the Moabites in 2 Chronicles chapter 20? "The battle is not yours but mine." Remember how our God works. He doesn't sleep nor slumber! When you are struggling, God is working things out that you can't see with the physical eye.

The key to your victory is to persevere. You don't know how close you are to your breakthrough!

God will show up and fight your battles when you put them in His hands. All we need do is wear the whole armor of God, stand strong, and pray, watch, and persevere, as Paul said in Ephesians 6:18.

You are an important member of the body of Christ! Victory in your life means victory for whole body! People will find a family of love, acceptance, power, redemption, and restoration—a church built on the Word of God and filled with His Spirit; a place people can experience salvation and blessings flowing.

The battle is not always easy, and at times, we become afflicted, but hold on to His Word. Remind yourself that the rough times are only for a season. As long as you stay in the house of the Lord and covered by His blood, you will be victorious through Christ.

> **2 Chronicles 20:15** *And he said, "Listen, all Judah and inhabitants of Jerusalem and King Jehoshaphat: Thus says the LORD to you, 'Do not be afraid and do not be dismayed at this great horde, for the battle is not yours but God's.'" (ESV)*

APPLICATION
Read:
Isaiah 41:11-13

Pray-That God will protect you from your enemies and that you will let God fight your battles, knowing that Hhe will always have the victory!

DAILY REFLECTION:
Do you find it difficult to let go and let God fight your battles? Why or why not?

DAY 15:

STRENGTHEN YOUR ARMOR!

W e have heard it preached on many occasions to "put on the whole armor of God," and rightfully so. However, I believe that sometimes putting on the armor of God is not enough.

After we have put it on, we need to identify any weaknesses or chinks it may have in order to strengthen it.

Have you ever seen the movie *The Last Samurai*[1] with Tom Cruise? Remember that scene early in the film when he is being attacked by the samurai and he's on the ground? He's able to jab the samurai in his neck, even with all the armor the samurai had on. This was because he had studied the samurai's armor and knew its weakness.[2]

That is what the devil wants to do to us. He wants to find that weakness in our armor and exploit it. He seeks to identify those areas of vulnerability that we have and use them to bring us down and separate us from God. That is why it is critical that we strengthen our armor.

We need to "self-police" ourselves, if you will, and identify those weak areas in our lives and work on improving them. If we make this a lifestyle in our walk with God, we will continue to strengthen our armor!

Ephesians: 6:10-18 *Finally, be strong in the Lord and in the strength of his might. ¹¹ Put on the whole armor of God, that you may be able to stand against the schemes of* the devil. [12] *For we do not wrestle against flesh and blood, but against the rulers, against the authorities, against the cosmic powers over this present darkness, against the spiritual forces of evil in the heavenly places.* [13] *Therefore take up the whole armor of God, that you may be able to withstand in the evil day, and having done all, to stand firm.* [14] *Stand therefore, having fastened on the belt of truth, and having put on the breastplate of righteousness,* [15] *and, as shoes for your feet, having put on the readiness given by the gospel of peace.* [16] *In all circumstances take up the shield of faith, with which you can extinguish all the flaming darts of the evil one;* [17] *and take the helmet of salvation, and the sword of the Spirit, which is the word of God,* [18] *praying at all times in the Spirit, with all prayer and supplication. To that end, keep alert with all perseverance, making supplication for all the saints.* (ESV)

APPLICATION
Read:
Hebrews 12:1
Ephesians 4:26-27

Pray-That God will strengthen your armor by revealing your weaknesses He wants to correct. Pray so you don't give the devil the foothold he wants to have in your life. Ask God to help you learn to "self-police" your thoughts and behaviors.

DAILY REFLECTION:
What does it look like for you to strengthen your armor?

DAY 16:
LET GOD FIGHT

Remember the story of David and Goliath, how Saul tried to give David his armor, according to 1 Samuel? We have always been told that the reason David did not wear Saul's armor was because he was too small for it. Just being a kid, it didn't fit him. But that is not what the Bible says. The Bible says that David did not wear Saul's armor because he hadn't proved it. That simply means he hadn't tested it yet. He had enough honor and respect for battle to know that he couldn't just wear someone else's armor that he himself hadn't gone to battle in.

So, what then was David's armor? It was the name of the Lord. This was his protection and covering.

You see, what David understood is that if you go into war, you must take the name of the Lord with you!

That is your protection! That is your covering! Not any physical armor, but God's covering.

David knew that it wasn't going to be by his own hand that he would defeat Goliath; it would be through the Lord. David remembered how God had delivered the lion and the bear to him. He had "proved" the name of the Lord in battle! (See 1 Samuel 17:36-37)

David was a man after God's own heart. He knew to give God the glory and the credit for defeating Goliath. When we go to war against the enemy, we must go in with the attitude that it is God who will fight our battle. And it is God who will bring the victory. Just like when Michael the archangel contested with Satan over the body of Moses. Michael said, "The Lord rebuke thee." (Jude 1:9) That must be our attitude in spiritual warfare, and we must have that same confidence to let God fight and give Him the glory!

1 Samuel 17:44-47 *The Philistine said to David, "Come to me, and I will give your flesh to the birds of the air and to the beasts of the field."* [45] *Then David said to the Philistine, "You come to me with a sword and with a spear and with a javelin, but I come to you in the name of the LORD of hosts, the God of the armies of Israel, whom you have defied.* [46] *This day the LORD will deliver you into my hand, and I will strike you down and cut off your head. And I will give the dead bodies of the host of the Philistines this day to the birds of the air and to the wild beasts of the earth that all the earth may know that there is a God in Israel,* [47] *and that all this assembly may know that the LORD saves not with sword and spear. For the battle is the LORD's, and he will give you into our hand." (ESV)*

APPLICATION
Read:
Proverbs 18:10
1 Samuel 17:36-40

Pray-That you will learn to let God fight your battles and that you will give Him the glory **before** the battle is won!

DAILY REFLECTION:
Have you ever been in a battle where you just stopped and let God fight? If so, what was the outcome? If not, do you think you could?

DAY 17:

ANOINTING FOR BATTLE

W e can all agree that Paul was a highly anointed vessel of God, right? Well, what is the first thing God said about him—not that he would be anointed or do great exploits, but what?

It was that he must suffer for Christ's namesake (Acts 9:16)

Anointing is not freely given by God; He gives His anointing very seriously for a specific period and does not grant it lightly. It is His virtue bestowed upon us so we can accomplish His will.

Did you know that you can be in sin and still have God's anointing? Don't believe me? Just look at Saul. In 1 Samuel, Saul was being haunted by evil spirits. He disobeyed God's commandment after the war with the Amalekites by not destroying everything as he had been told and continually tried to kill David. That sounds like sin to me. Yet by the time we get to 1 Samuel 24, David had the perfect opportunity to kill Saul, and he refused, saying, "I will not touch God's anointed." As I said before, God's anointing is not something we should take lightly. We should honor and protect it, and one way to do that is to pay attention to our armor.

I did some research on armor as I was preparing this work. Here's what I discovered. Armor has gone through many transformations throughout the years. It started out as a leather covering, changed to chain mail, and then transformed to steel and stronger metals. Nowadays, Kevlar is used to protect our military and police. However, what do all these materials have in common? They all contain weaknesses. The enemy goes for the weakest points, such as the joints and the eyes—be careful what you look at. Protect that anointing that God has given you!

1 Samuel 24:1-7 *When Saul returned from following the Philistines, he was told, "Behold, David is in the wilderness of Engedi." Then Saul took three thousand chosen men out of all Israel and went to seek David and his men in front of the Wildgoats' Rocks. And he came to the sheepfolds by the way, where there was a cave, and Saul went in to relieve himself. Now David and his men were sitting in the innermost parts of the cave. 4And the men of David said to him, "Here is the day of which the LORD said to you, 'Behold, I will give your enemy into your hand, and you shall do to him as it shall seem good to you.'" Then David arose and stealthily cut off a corner of Saul's robe. And afterward David's heart struck him, because he had cut off a corner of Saul's robe. He said to his men, "The LORD forbid that I should do this thing to my lord, the LORD's anointed, to put out my hand against him, seeing he is the LORD's anointed." So David persuaded his men with these words and did not permit them to attack Saul. And Saul rose up and left the cave and went on his way. (ESV)*

Application
Read:
Acts 9:16
1 Samuel 26:6-12

Pray-That God will give you His anointing to protect you and keep you in battle, even if it means you have to suffer for His namesake.

Daily Reflection:
How important do you think God's anointing is in your life and in the area of spiritual warfare? What have you been anointed to do for Him?

DAY 18:

The Sword of the Spirit: Your Offense

The sword is our attacking piece of armor. Aren't you glad that God made it plain through Paul's writing what the sword of the Spirit is? It is the Word of God, and there is no better weapon to combat the enemy!

Remember Jesus's example? He was in the garden of Gethsemane and had just come off forty days of fasting. The enemy came to Him, tempting Him three times. Each time, Jesus reopened by making the same statement to start His rebuttal.

"It is written, it is written, it is written!"

What a great example for us as believers today! We can use God's Word to reject and refute Satan when he attacks us!

Using the Word of God not only toward the enemy but in every aspect of our lives is a powerful weapon that no one can withstand!

That is why we must know the Word, read the Word, hear the Word, and speak the Word.

Finally, studying God's Word will help us keep our sword strong and sharp.

Matthew 4:1-11 *Then Jesus was led up by the Spirit into the wilderness to be tempted by the devil. ² And after fasting forty days and forty nights, he was hungry. ³ And the tempter came and said to him, "If you are the Son of God, command these stones to become loaves of bread." ⁴ But he answered, "It is written, "'Man shall not live by bread alone, but by every word that comes from the mouth of God." ⁵ Then the devil took him to the holy city and set him on the pinnacle of the temple ⁶ and said to him, "If you are the Son of God, throw yourself down, for it is written, "'He will command his angels concerning you, 'and "'On their hands they will bear you up, lest you strike your foot against a stone.'" ⁷ Jesus said to him, "Again it is written, 'You shall not put the Lord your God to the test.'" ⁸ Again, the devil took him to a very high mountain and showed him all the kingdoms of the world and their glory. ⁹ And he said to him, "All these I will give you, if you will fall down and worship me." ¹⁰ Then Jesus said to him, "Be gone, Satan! For it is written, You shall worship the Lord your God and him only shall you serve.'" ¹¹ Then the devil left him, and behold, angels came and were ministering to him. (ESV)*

APPLICATION
Read:
Hebrews 4:12
2 Timothy 2:15

Pray-That God will use His Word to show you imperfections you can work on. Pray that He will give you a deep love for His Word so you can study it and use it as a formidable weapon against the enemy and anything contrary to God you may be facing.

DAILY REFLECTION:
How has this devotional helped you realize how powerful the Word can be as a weapon in your life?

DAY 19:

A WILLING MIND:
YOUR DEFENSE

G od has given us all the spiritual armor that we need. It is up to us to maintain it and keep it strong. It starts with our loins being girded with truth. Truth in Christ is a basic tenet of our walk with God. We must know Him and know the truth His Word gives us, our salvation.

Then we wear the breastplate of righteousness, our right standing with God. We ensure we are in a place of acceptance with Him. We must have our lives cleansed and holy before God.

Wherever you go, you should also take the peace of God with you. Take the gospel of good news, and as the Word says, "Follow peace with all men…" (Hebrews 12:14).

We also put on our shield of faith, which is our belief in God and one of the most important aspects of our armor. Remember Abraham? The Bible tells us that he believed God and it was counted to him as righteousness (Romans 4:3). Your faith in God is a major part of your armor—it covers your chest.

A shield protects against swords and spears and the fiery darts of the enemy (Ephesians 6:16). This is what I love about this passage in Ephesians and this particular piece of armor. Our shield of faith doesn't simply "put out" the devil's fiery darts; it quenches them. (Ephesians 6:16) In other words, the shield of faith will completely douse the fiery darts so they have no chance of lighting again and coming back. They will be quenched forever. We ought not to go to battle without our shield of faith.

And then there's the helmet of salvation to protect our heads and our minds. We've heard it before, that the battle takes place in our minds. It's where fear, doubt, and unbelief can grow and where suspicion, uncertainty, and pessimism can live. But it is also the place where faith, belief, and action start and where a positive attitude and a clear perspective can thrive!

So much of what we become in our lives for Christ starts in our minds. It starts with our thinking, and how we allow God to change our thinking makes us more like Him.

What you think tends to become what you believe, and what you believe becomes who you are.

If you want to change your life, change your thinking!

You must have a progressive mentality to live a successful life in God as well as *a willing mind*—one willing to see things the way God sees them to be able to live for Him. Our minds are critical to our salvation. Everything we are starts here; that is why God gives us a helmet, to cover our minds. We must put it on and be sure to strengthen any weakness in it.

Philippians 4:8 *Finally, brothers, whatever is true, whatever is honorable, whatever is just, whatever is pure, whatever is lovely, whatever is commendable, if there is any excellence, if there is anything worthy of praise, think about these things. (ESV)*

APPLICATION
Read:
Romans 12:2
Philippians 2:1-4

Pray-That God will help you develop a mind like His and see things from His perspective.

DAILY REFLECTION:
Spiritual warfare starts in the mind. In what ways can you prepare your mind for this battle?

DAY 20:

THE GREATEST VIRTUE

You know when we talk of the armor of God, we always refer to Ephesians 6, and rightly so. But did you know that this is not the only scripture that speaks of our spiritual armor? When we look over the virtues of our spiritual armor, what seems to be missing?

We have truth, righteousness, peace, faith, and salvation. But what is the most powerful virtue of them all?

First Corinthians chapter 13 tells us it is love.

Our breastplate is to protect our hearts. And we find out also that the helmet is more than just used to protect our minds. It is also a place for our hope—the hope we have in our salvation, our hope that we have a better world waiting for us.

Be encouraged, friend. You have a great hope in the world that is to come where Jesus reigns, prepared for us because He loved us enough to die on the cross and in doing so, provided a way to be reconciled and spend eternity with Him. What a blessed hope shown by the love He has for us.

Yet before we get there, we must realize that there are spiritual battles and trials we must endure. Again, we have hope because of the spiritual armor God has given us. We must be prepared to fight. But be of good courage—our Lord has never lost a battle.

1 Corinthians 13:13 *So now faith, hope, and love abide, these three; but the greatest of these is love. (ESV)*

APPLICATION
Read:
1 Thessalonians 5:8
Proverbs 10:12
1 Peter 4:8
1 Corinthians 13

Pray-That you will be intentional about putting on your spiritual armor every day. Pray that you will have the peace to know you can rest in the hope of salvation God has provided for you.

DAILY REFLECTION:
Simply put, what does God's love mean to you?

THE KING HAS ONE MORE MOVE
(DAYS 21-24)

There is no other story in the Bible which communicates the spiritual battle that takes over our lives better than the story of Job. We will cover this in the next five days of our devotional. And we'll cover it from God's viewpoint, as well as the game of chess.

Ever hear the story about the checkmate painting?

In 1831, Moritz August Retzsch, a German painter and etcher, painted a well-known masterpiece called *Checkmate* (originally titled *Die Schachspieler* "The Chess Players")[3]. In the painting, a man is playing chess with the devil. The devil is staring at the young man, who has his hand on his head in obvious defeat because the devil has him trapped. The title of the painting, *Checkmate*, indicates that the game is over. The devil has won, and the young man's king is in peril. He has no more moves.

Two men were walking through an art gallery admiring a famous painting. After seeing the painting, the first man wanted to move on to other paintings in the gallery. But the second man, an international chess champion, wanted to look at the painting longer, so he waved his friend on and told him he would catch up later.

The chess champion stared and stared at the chessboard and then suddenly stepped back, flabbergasted. "It's wrong!" he exclaimed. "There's one more move!" He ran to his friend, and together they looked at the painting. "We have to contact the painter," the chess champion said. "It's not checkmate. *The king has one more move!*"

As you are about to discover in our study of Job, when you feel like the devil has you defeated, know this: with God on your side, the game is *never* over. Our King has one more move!

DAY 21:

GOD'S VICTORY OVER SATAN THROUGH THE LIFE OF JOB

We know that the devil, as a roaring lion, goes about seeking whom he may devour. We know he hates us for taking his place and will do whatever he can to hinder us and steal from us.

We also know that God always has the victory, and with Him on our side, we will triumph over the enemy. God will take what the devil meant for evil and turn it into good for our lives.

There is no better example of this in the Bible than the book of Job. God told me some time ago to read Job, and as I did, He began to open my eyes to some things. He showed me how He used the devil's tactics against him and how He had everything in control in Job's life.

In Job 1:7, we see that God was expecting Satan to be there when the angels came to present themselves. He asked Satan sarcastically, "Whence comest thou?" (KJV)

God knew what he was up to and already had His plan in place.

So, Satan started telling God all about the good things He had done for Job, including putting a hedge about him, his family, and all that he had. It is obvious Satan wanted God to remove that hedge so he could attack.

You know what happens to a hedge when you cut it? It grows back higher!

Now, this is the part I really like—verse 11. Satan told God to put forth His hand and touch all that Job had and that Job would curse God to His face.

Now, how many of you know that the hand of the Lord is used for creation and is a place of power and blessing?

So what Satan was doing when he told God to put forth His hand and touch all that Job had was telling God to bless him! It's as if Satan forgot who he was talking to!

When God's hand touches you, it will always bring blessing, protection, and victory!

> **Job 1: 6-11** *Now there was a day when the sons of God came to present themselves before the LORD, and Satan[b] also came among them. ⁷ The LORD said to Satan, "From where have you come?" Satan answered the LORD and said, "From going to and fro on the earth, and from walking up and down on it." ⁸ And the LORD said to Satan, "Have you considered my servant Job, that there is none like him on the earth, a blameless and upright man, who fears God and turns away from evil?" ⁹ Then Satan answered the LORD and said, "Does Job fear God for no reason? ¹⁰ Have you not put a hedge around him and his house and all that he has, on every side? You have blessed the work of his hands, and his possessions have increased in the land. ¹¹ But stretch out your hand and touch all that he has, and he will curse you to your face." (ESV)*

Application
Read:
Exodus 15:6
Psalms 37:23-24
Psalms 98:1

Pray-That God will keep His hand upon you and bring you out of any tribulation the enemy tries to throw your way. Pray that you will have a fresh revelation of the power of God's hand on your life.

Daily Reflection:
How does it make you feel knowing that God was in control in His dealings with Satan the entire time?

DAY 22:

GOD IS IN CONTROL

W e give the devil so much credit when he doesn't even know what God has planned for us! He didn't know what God was going to do for Job, or else he wouldn't have gone after him, just like he didn't know Jesus was going to rise from the dead! Satan doesn't know all; only God does. So, God will always have the upper hand on him! Praise God!

We know from Matthew 28:18 that Jesus has all power in heaven and earth, so the only power Satan has in your life (or Job's) is what God allows him to have.

Now, I want you to get this! God will allow Satan to mess with your stuff so that when you continue to live righteously and not curse Him, He will give it all back to you and more—you will be blessed, and He will get the glory!

In this game of chess, Satan can only move when and how God tells him. In the grand scheme of things for you and me, he is only a pawn; God holds the true power. Now notice that when the term "a day" is used in verse 13, it is referring to our time, human time. But when "a day" is used in verse 6, it is referring to God's time. The verses show a cycle of repetition in the words they use, but one is God's clock, while the other is man's clock.

Now verse 14 says a messenger came to Job to tell him what had happened. A messenger in the Bible is someone who is sent from God, like Gabriel was a messenger sent to Mary or John was a messenger sent to tell of the coming of Jesus.

God allowed a messenger to survive to tell Job what was happening. It was as if God was giving Job a heads up, letting him know what was coming.

God's always in the midst of your trouble, even when you don't realize it.

Now in verse 16, the Bible says, "The fire of God fell from Heaven." The fire of God in 1 Kings 18:36-38 was God's answer to Elijah's prayer; in Acts 2, it was the Holy Spirit falling in the upper room as the disciples were praying in unity.

Fire of God falling from heaven is a sign that God is responding to a certain situation or prayer. Perhaps Job started praying to God as soon as this calamity hit? In any case, I believe it was a sign to Job that God was allowing this to happen and that if Job could trust God, everything would be alright.

Surely Job understood this for no man could endure what he did and still worship God without a sign from God to say, "I'm in control; I'm still here."

Job 1:13-16 *¹³Now there was a day when his sons and daughters were eating and drinking wine in their oldest brother's house, ¹⁴and there came a messenger to Job and said, "The oxen were plowing and the donkeys feeding beside them, ¹⁵and the Sabeans fell upon them and took them and struck down the servantsᶜ with the edge of the sword, and I alone have escaped to tell you." ¹⁶While he was yet speaking, there came another and said, "The fire of God fell from heaven and burned up the sheep and the servants and consumed them, and I alone have escaped to tell you." (ESV)*

APPLICATION
Read:
1 Kings 18:36-38
Acts 2:1-4

Pray-That you will be able to withstand any tragedy or trial that comes your way and that you will lean into God with an unfailing trust, knowing He has a bigger plan for your life.

DAILY REFLECTION:
How does it make you feel to know that no matter what you go through, God is always in control?

DAY 22:

WORSHIP IN DISTRESS

We need to understand that no matter what we go through when we are facing disasters and our world is crashing all around us, God has not forsaken us. He is still right there, even if we can't feel Him.

If we trust Him and continue to do right (see Job 1:11), He will show up and restore all that we have lost.

Now notice where Job's children were in verse 18 when the attack hit. They were in their eldest brother's house. You see, Satan always wants to attack from the top, taking out the eldest, the leadership, if you will.

Verses 15-19 all have more cycles of repetition—they all use the term "I only," and verses 16-18 all say "while he was yet speaking." I believe these messengers with their consistent speech were a sign from God letting Job know that even while all hell was breaking loose around him, He was still there.

Verse 19 gives us yet another sign that God is holding the puppet strings: a great wind came. In Acts chapter 2, a great wind was a sign of the coming Holy Spirit.

Understand that the devil was destroying all that Job had, but he was doing it with signs that God was allowing him to use. Fire and wind are elements that come from God, not the devil.

God was simply relinquishing power to the devil, allowing him to work, but saying to Job: "I'm right here. I haven't gone anywhere."

What an awesome God we serve!

Also, notice in verse 19 that the devil attacked the four corners of the house, the foundation.

The enemy wants to shake your foundation and bring it down because no building can stand without one.

Without a strong foundation in Jesus, we will fall at the first sign of trouble.

The key to a long, successful walk with God is to start from a firm foundation. Build it on Him, His Word, worship and prayer, faithfulness to the house of God, and meat for His house, your giving.

These are things that will make your foundation strong and allow you to withstand the attack of the enemy.

Now let's look at the rest of verse 19. Notice who the enemy attacked—the young men, our future generation. The enemy would love to steal our children, and he will do everything he can to hinder them. If he can't get us, he will go after the future of the church.

Now verse 20—this is the most important verse in the first chapter because this is where Job fits in, and we can learn from his example. Job's purpose became clear in his mind, and he knew what he had to do. The Bible says that he fell upon the ground and worshipped. What an awesome example of *worship* in distress!

When the devil pulls out all the stops against you, if you worship God and don't sin, you'll put the devil in check, and checkmate will be just around the corner.

Job 1:18-21 While he was yet speaking, there came another and said, "Your sons and daughters were eating and drinking wine in their oldest brother's house, ¹⁹and behold, a great wind came across the wilderness and struck the four corners of the house, and it fell upon the young people, and they are dead, and I alone have escaped to tell you." ²⁰Then Job arose and tore his robe and shaved his head and fell on the ground and worshiped. And he said ²¹"Naked I came from my mother's womb, and naked shall I return. The LORD gave, and the LORD has taken away; blessed be the name of the LORD." (ESV)

APPLICATION

Read:
Job 13:15
Psalms 34:1-7
Matthew 7:24-25

Pray-That God's hand will be upon our leadership and our children. Plead the blood of Christ over them. Pray that God will protect them and keep them and that in times of distress, He will give you the strength to worship like Job did.

DAILY REFLECTION:
Have you found it difficult to worship the Lord in times of trouble? Why or why not? How can worshipping the Lord in distress change the outcome? Have you experienced this in your life?

DAY 24:

CHECKMATE

N ow Job chapter 2 starts with the cycle all over again, and God really had the devil frustrated. Can't you just hear the sarcasm in verse 2? "Where ya been, Satan?" God knew and as usual, He had Satan all turned around and was one step ahead of him.

Get this—in verse 3, God repeated His description of Job as a perfect and upright man to Satan, but notice what He did. He added another compliment to Job—He said that Job was one who held fast to his integrity.

You see, God will take notice of how you react to trials in your life, and He will defend you in the face of the enemy. If you keep your character and attitude right, when Satan returns to God about you, God will let him know what kind of man or woman you are, and He will come to your defense when Satan wants to attack.

Notice also that the Lord said that there was no cause to go after Job. When you're doing right and the world crashes around you, your victory is just around the corner.

In verse 6, God told Satan to save Job's life. Remember, God will only let your trial go so far. He knows just how far you can go and what you can handle. God will only bring you home when your purpose has been fulfilled. Job's purpose was to worship and be an example. God spared him because his purpose was not finished.

God in His mercy put the story of Job in the Bible so we could see that He is always in control and to testify to the world that the devil can never win and doesn't really have power over us. His only power is relinquished from God and ultimately will serve to strengthen us and glorify God.

At the end of the story, we find Job realizing that God was in control and repenting to Him for his change of attitude when he did curse the day he had been born.

And the Bible says the Lord blessed the latter of Job more than his beginning.(Job 42:12)

No matter what you go through or what Satan throws your way, you can rest assured knowing that God is in control. He will give you the victory, and He will get the glory in the end.

God will always put the devil in checkmate.

> **Job 2:1-3,6** *Again there was a day when the sons of God came to present themselves before the LORD, and Satan also came among them to present himself before the LORD. ²And the LORD said to Satan, "From where have you come?" Satan answered the LORD and said, "From going to and fro on the earth, and from walking up and down on it." ³And the LORD said to Satan, "Have you considered my servant Job, that there is none like him on the earth, a blameless and upright man, who fears God and turns away from evil? He still holds fast his integrity, although you incited me against him to destroy him without reason."*
>
> *⁶And the LORD said to Satan, "Behold, he is in your hand; only spare his life." (ESV)*

APPLICATION
Read:
Job 42:1-6, 12-17
Psalms 1:1-3

Pray-That you will maintain the right attitude toward God while you wait for the victory. If you find need to repent, repent. Pray that you will trust Him and that you will see Him in new light, like Job did.

DAILY REFLECTION:
What comfort do you have in knowing the end of Job's story and how God blessed him with more than he originally had?

TO FORGIVE AND BE FORGIVEN (DAYS 25-27)

We've all been there before. Think back to a time when someone hurt you badly: a close relative or friend, perhaps, or even a church member. Remember how hard it was to forgive that person, or maybe you still haven't forgiven him or her. How did (or does) holding on to that pain make you feel? How did (or can) forgiving this person change your life?

As you read through the next three days, I pray that you will learn some things about forgiveness that perhaps you never knew. You can put the application of forgiveness into your life in a practical way while exercising any bitterness and hurt out. We know that basis of our or religion is based on God's love for us and how that love bought us salvation and forgiveness of our sins. I hope that when you are done with the next few days, you too will be able to better receive the forgiveness God has for you and in doing so grant forgiveness along to those in your life who need it.

It is critical that you learn to accept your own forgiveness and in turn forgive those around you. Once you do, you will experience a newfound freedom that will bring joy and peace to your life, and you will also grow to become more like Him.

DAY 25:

LOVE AND FORGIVENESS

W hen we think of Christ and what He did for us and all that encompasses this Christlike walk, it all boils down to one thing: love. Love is the basis of everything that God did for us. We are all familiar with this popular scripture. It's written on signs at sporting events, bumper stickers, T-shirts, etc. Do you know what scripture I'm referencing? John 3:16: "For God so loved the world..."

John had a better understanding of this than anyone else in the Scriptures as evidenced by how much he wrote about it. As a matter of fact, he conveyed to us in his letters that love is the very essence of who God is. See 1 John 4:8.

First John 4 could very well be called the "love chapter," just like we refer to 1 Corinthians 13 as that. If you read through 1 John 4, you'll get a clearer understanding of what it means to love God and to be loved by God. Verse 10: He loved us. Verse 12: His love is made complete in us. Verse 18: There is no fear in love. Verse 19: He first loved us.

Love is essential in understanding what Christ did for us. And His love for us led Him to give of Himself and ultimately forgive us. We must also learn to apply love in this manner. It's not simply loving others; it's what loving others will result in and lead you to do—forgive! There is a freeing power in the act of forgiveness, which we will look at in more detail. When you think about the cross, you understand that Jesus's death was all about forgiveness. We know that without the shedding of blood there is no remission of sins (Hebrews 9:22). Not only were your sins remitted, but you were forgiven! Oh, the power in forgiveness!

Love and forgiveness are at the very core of our walk with God.

Matthew 22:37-40 *And he said to him, "You shall love the Lord your God with all your heart and with all your soul and with all your mind. ³⁸ This is the great and first commandment. ³⁹ And a second is like it: You shall love your neighbor as yourself. ⁴⁰ On these two commandments depend all the Law and the Prophets." (ESV)*

Luke 23:33-34 *And when they came to the place that is called The Skull, there they crucified him, and the criminals, one on his right and one on his left. ³⁴ And Jesus said, "Father, forgive them, for they know not what they do."[a] And they cast lots to divide his garments. (ESV)*

APPLICATION
Read:
Matthew 6:12, 14-15
Matthew 18:21-22

Pray-That God will give you a fresh perspective and understanding of His love for us and that you will recognize that His love led to your forgiveness so you, in turn, can forgive others.

DAILY REFLECTION:
Explain in your own words how love and forgiveness are intertwined.

DAY 26:

THE POWER OF FORGIVENESS

O n our previous day, I shared how God's love for us led to His forgiveness for us. Now let's look at just how powerful forgiveness can be as you apply it to others.

Psalms 103:12 and Micah 7:19 tell us how powerful forgiveness is. God told us that He casts our sins so far away that we can't even comprehend it!

Forgiveness is a dynamic action for both the forgiver and the offender. Think back to the last time you felt mercy, the forgiveness of God in your life. Maybe it was yesterday or even today. How did you feel? Grateful? Clean? Changed? Free? Did you feel a sense of calm, perhaps even joy? Doesn't it feel good to know that God has forgiven you?

Being forgiven by God is the easy part. In 1 John 1:9, we read that if we confess our sins, He is faithful and just to forgive us. Receiving God's forgiveness is not difficult. We already read that His shedding of blood made it possible for us.

The act of forgiveness toward others is the real challenge. It's one thing to ask our Heavenly Father for forgiveness, but it's more difficult for us as to extend the same forgiveness to others. Jesus in His infinite wisdom is our perfect example. In Luke 23:34, Jesus said, "Father, forgive them." What a model for us! Have any of us ever experienced a crown of thorns put on our heads or been forced to drink vinegar? Or carried a heavy cross on a bloody, wounded back? Of course not, yet Jesus asked His Father to forgive us. Wow, what a powerful image!

If Jesus could go through all of that and still pray for forgiveness for others, how much more should we be willing to forgive? Christ is certainly our example, but there's more to it than that. Do you realize that how you treat others has a bearing on how God treats you?

> **Matthew: 6:12,14-15** ...*And forgive us our debts, as we also have forgiven our debtors.* [14] *For if you forgive others their trespasses, your heavenly Father will also forgive you,* [15] *but if you do not forgive others their trespasses, neither will your Father forgive your trespasses.* (ESV)

APPLICATION
Read:
Psalms 103:12
Micah 7:19

Pray-Ask God to search your heart for people you need to forgive; then willfully make the decision to do so. Ask Him to give you the strength, and that strength will become part of your continual walk with God.

DAILY REFLECTION:
Why do you think forgiveness is such a powerful aspect of our Christian walk?

DAY 27:

5 PRINCIPLES OF FORGIVENESS

As we wrap up our section on forgiveness, I'd like to give you five principles that will help and encourage you. Take these to heart, and they will help you with this life-changing action.

1. There is no limit to God's forgiveness. Read Matthew 18:21-22. God's forgiveness is not a license to sin but our reassurance that when we mess up, He is there with an open heart to love and forgive us.
2. When you don't forgive others, you hurt yourself. You risk not receiving God's forgiveness (Matthew 6:15) and growing cold inside. How can we have peace while holding grudges and unforgiveness in our hearts? The Word also tells us that the root of bitterness can spring up, and we can become defiled(Hebrews 12:15).
3. True forgiveness is made possible only by the blood of Jesus. The Bible tells us there is no remission without the shedding of blood (Hebrews 9:22). Exodus 29:36 speaks of the animal sacrifices that were used to atone for sins. Leviticus chapters 1-7 discusses specific sacrifices and the sprinkling of blood. How much more does the precious blood of God's only Son blot out our transgressions? Oh, what power in the blood!
4. Forgiveness is a conscience choice, a willing decision. You must make up your mind and heart that you are going to extend forgiveness to someone. It does not always come easily. There is an action that must take place when forgiveness is offered. Our flesh will often hold on to the grudge as a victim. Some feel a sense

of power when they hold on to the decision to forgive or not. We know in our hearts that the right action is always to forgive while maintaining our access to God's mercy. The release and freedom that you will experience is so beautiful!

5. One cannot truly forgive without God's help. It's not in our carnal nature, but the Holy Spirit will help us. If you feel that you may not be in a place to extend forgiveness yet, pray and ask for strength. William Blake said, "It is easier to forgive an enemy than a friend;"[4]. That should not be true for a Christian. Luke 6:37 reads, "Forgive and be forgiven." God requires us to forgive others; therefore, He will help us to do so if we ask Him.

As difficult as forgiveness may be, don't allow bitterness and anger to take hold in your spirit. It will eventually control and destroy you. Choose to forgive! The good news is that the power of forgiveness will bring healing and freedom to your life. Forgiveness is more for you than for the person who needs it.

2 Chronicles 7:14 *If my people who are called by my name humble themselves, and pray and seek my face and turn from their wicked ways, then I will hear from heaven and will forgive their sin and heal their land. (ESV)*

Application
Read:
Matthew 18:21-22
Hebrews 12:14-15
2 Chronicles 7:14

Pray-That God will help you understand the importance of forgiveness and how you can ask the Holy Spirit to help you to forgive. Remember that you cannot truly forgive in your power. It's not something that you can do in your flesh.

Daily Reflection:
What have you learned from these lessons on forgiveness that you can apply today? Who in your life do you need to forgive? What steps will you take to forgive them?

THE 3:16'S
(DAYS 28-31)

Some years ago as I was studying the Word, I came across the revelation that there are a number of "3:16" verses in the Bible that stand out, and when sown together, they can form a great picture of God's love and sacrifice for us.

At the time, I thought nothing more of it, but as I was putting this work together, those thoughts came back to me.

I believe the Lord wanted me to include my discovery in this book, so for the next four days, I have included four 3:16 verses for you that weave a beautiful story together, showing just how much God loves us. I pray that as you reach the end of this devotional, you'll find a sense of wonder and gratitude in what God did for us by sending His Son and what Christ did for us by dying on the cross.

If you find this book to be a blessing to you, pass it along and share it as gift to someone you know.

May God richly bless you and all that you set out to accomplish for Him!!

DAY 28:

JOHN

I t used to be that you would be watching a football game and you would see the verse on a poster or two in the stands. Or perhaps you would ask someone who may not claim to be a believer what his or her knowledge of Scripture is and invariably would get this response: "John 3:16!" It is the universally known verse of Scripture whether someone knows the Bible or not.

Let's discuss why this is the case.

The gospel of John, written by the apostle John, has as part of its purpose the revelation of Jesus as the Son of God. In this gospel, Jesus gave a more complete revelation of Himself than in the synoptic gospels. For example, in John, we learn more about the divinity of Jesus, the work of the Holy Spirit, and of God the Father than anywhere else in the Bible. Jesus spoke of God as "The Father" over *100* times in this gospel!

So, what is it about this verse that makes it so popular? Let's take a look: in chapter 3 of the gospel of John, we see a Pharisee and ruler of the Jews named Nicodemus. In this passage, Nicodemus comes to Jesus at night and acknowledges He was a teacher come from God. (John 3:2) Immediately Jesus tells Nicodemus that he must be born again. Unfortunately, Nicodemus heard this in a carnal way, responding, "How can a man be born when he is old?" (John 3:4). Fortunately for Nicodemus, Jesus continued to engage him by revealing a little more in their conversation. Still, Nicodemus was unsure and asked Jesus in verse 9, "How can these things be?" Jesus then took His time and for the next twelve verses unpacked what salvation looks like to Nicodemus, and right in the middle of Jesus's message is that ever-present, powerful verse we all know so well—3:16.

John 3:16, so powerful. Here is what stands out to me: God "so loves…" He gave "only…"

And "whosever…"

God loved the world so much He was willing to give His only Son for it, and "whosoever believes in him would not perish but have everlasting life." God's love for us became an act of giving for us. I am so thankful He loves us so much!

> **John 3:16** *"For God so loved the world,[i] that he gave his only Son, that whoever believes in him should not perish but have eternal life." (ESV)*

APPLICATION
Read:
John 3:3-8, 14-18
John 10:9-11

Pray-That God will give you a fresh revelation of His love for you so you can be confident in your identity and bold in His love as you share it with the world.

DAILY REFLECTION:
How does this devotional shape the way you think about your call from God to be a witness for Him?

DAY 29:
1 TIMOTHY

The first mention we have of Timothy in Scripture is found in Acts chapter 16. Luke, the writer of Acts, tells us that Timothy was a disciple when Paul met him in Lystra. The Bible also tells us that Timothy's mother was a Jew who believed, and his father was a Greek. Timothy had a good reputation by those who knew him, both in Lystra and Iconium (Acts 16:2).

Paul desired to have Timothy join him on his missionary journeys, but because his father was Greek, Paul circumcised him first. The Bible goes on to tell us that Paul and Timothy went though many cities and set up churches that were established in the faith and saw their numbers increase daily. Timothy eventually settled as the overseer of the church at Ephesus, as sent by Paul.

The second "3:16" verse we study comes from the book of 1 Timothy. As Paul grew fond of Timothy and mentioned him as his "son in the faith," he wrote two letters to Timothy that provided counsel and instruction to the young bishop. First Timothy can be broken down into five parts: 1) doctrinal assertions, 2) prayer and counsel to men and women, 3) spiritual oversight, 4) future predictions, and 5) ministerial administration.

It is in the third section of spiritual oversight that we find this particular 3:16 verse. "And without controversy." There is no question about what God has done for us. It is steadfast, true, and undeniable. Paul explained it in six facets: 1) God was manifest in flesh—that is, He came in the form of His Son. The

Word was made flesh and dwelt among us. 2) He was a justified in the Spirit. His work on earth was justified, and He was raised by the Spirit. 3) Jesus was seen of angels (the angels witnessed His work on earth and worshipped Him as well) (Heb. 1:6). 4) He preached unto the Gentiles. He came to seek and to save that which was lost, not only for Israel but for us too. 5) He was believed on in the world. Many of the Gentiles who heard Him preach believed on Him and were converted. 6) He was received up into glory. Jesus's ascension put Him at the right hand of God in a place of power and authority, where He makes intercession for us.

Paul stated this mystery of godliness then proceeded to break it down and explain it. In doing so, he gives us a better understanding of what Christ has done for us. For that we should all be thankful!

> **1 Timothy 3:16** And *without controversy great is the mystery of godliness: God was manifest in the flesh, justified in the Spirit, seen of angels, preached unto the Gentiles, believed on in the world, received up into glory. (ESV)*

APPLICATION
Read:
John 1:1,14

Pray-That God will continue to give you a deeper understanding of the gospel. Ask Him for a spirit of thankfulness for all He has done for you.

DAILY REFLECTION:
How does 1 Timothy 3:16 shape your understanding of the gospel? Does it help equip you to better share it with others now? Why or why not?

DAY 30:
2 TIMOTHY

P aul continued his exhortation and instruction in his second letter to Timothy. Paul wrote 2 Timothy from Rome between AD 65 and 67, and it contains his last recorded words.

Paul wrote this epistle for two purposes. The first was to continue to encourage and instruct Timothy as the young pastor was learning to minister. The second was to request that Timothy come to Rome so Paul could enjoy his fellowship. Paul was in prison, soon to be executed, and desired Timothy's presence for companionship.

In 2 Timothy chapter 3, Paul started by telling of the wickedness that would come in the future and encouraged Timothy to continue in what he had learned. Paul reminded Timothy of his knowledge of the Scriptures that he had gotten from a young age. Then Paul wrote that well-known verse: 3:16

Let's look at what the verse tells us: 2 Timothy 3:16 can be broken down into two subjects with some subcategories. The first statement is Paul's declaration that all Scripture is God inspired. That is, it must be understood that the entire Bible is "God-breathed." The second main point is that Bible providers benefit in multiple ways: doctrine, reproof, correction, and instruction in righteousness. Let's look briefly at each of these:

Doctrine: The Bible is profitable in helping us understand the tenants of God, His will, and how He provides salvation.

Reproof: The Bible will rebuke us when we make mistakes, which leads us to:

Correction: The Bible helps us to learn right from wrong so we don't stay in a place of shame. Finally,

Instruction in Righteousness: We are taught in righteous behavior, so after the reproof and correction, we can be in right standing with God!

It can be painful to look into the Word of God and measure our behavior against it. But when we allow it to correct and instruct us, it becomes profitable. That is good for our walk with God!

2 Timothy 3:16 All scripture is given by inspiration of God, and is profitable for doctrine, for reproof, for correction, for instruction in righteousness: (ESV)

APPLICATION
Read:
2 Timothy 3:17
2 Peter 1:20,21

Pray-That you will have the right attitude when God's Word corrects you. Pray for a teachable spirit so you can learn from His Word and become more like Him.

DAILY REFLECTION:
How has the Word of God been a reproof and a correction in your life? In turn, how can you use the Word to gently reproof and correct those you may be discipling?

DAY 31:

1 John

O ur final devotional and 3:16 verse is 1 John. As the apostle John wrote the gospel of John along with 1, 2, and 3 John, it would stand to reason that he conveyed many of the same messages throughout these writings. First John 3:16 is no exception.

The fundamental basis of our Christian religion is the message of God's love for us and what He did to demonstrate that love. He laid down His life for us. John 3:16 makes that clear, as does 1 John 3:16.

Here, however, John goes further as he challenges us to lay down our lives for our brothers (and sisters). This can mean a sacrifice of love so strong even of physical death, if needed. It also means to self-sacrifice and put others before ourselves. If we do not have to die physically for our spiritual family, the next best thing we can do is serve and sacrifice for them. (See 1 John 3:17-18) If we continually put others before ourselves, we will be fulfilling this scripture to the best of our ability.

The most important aspect to understand from this 3:16 scripture is to realize just how much God loves us! And when we understand and appreciate that He loves us so much that He was willing to lay down His life for us, in doing so, Jesus provides the opportunity for us to experience relationship with Him here on earth and salvation forevermore. We not only have the privilege of knowing Him here on earth but for eternity too. That is the good news of His story for us and one we should share with everyone who does not know Him!

1 John 3:16: *By this we know love, that he laid down His life for us, and we out to lay down our lives for our brothers.* *(ESV)*

APPLICATION
Read:
John 15:13
Matthew 22:37-39
Mark 12:30

Pray-That we will have a sacrificial heart to serve others and put them before ourselves and in doing so, become more Christ-like.

DAILY REFLECTION:
As you come to the end of the book, take some time to reflect on what you have learned about God's love for you, as that theme has been weaved throughout this devotional. How will that change the way you live your life?

Journal

REFERENCES:

1. Wikipedia Online "delayed gratification" accessed February 5th 2020 https://en.wikipedia.org/wiki/Delayed_gratification

2. Zwick, Edward, director. 2003 *The Last Samurai.* Warner Bros.

3. ONE-MORE-MOVE-CHESSART.COM Bronze Bas Relief Masterprice and Background Story-The King Has One More Move! The "One More Move" Story of Paul Morphy and The Moritz Retzsch Painting 2015. https://www.one-more-move-chess-art.com/One-More-Move.html

4. Cheryl Lavin, "It is easier to forgive an enemy...." Chicago Tribune June 7. 1998. Accessed June 5,2021 https://www.chicagotribune.com/news/ct-xpm-1998-06-07-9806070287-story.html

CPSIA information can be obtained
at www.ICGtesting.com
Printed in the USA
BVHW060035010921
615695BV00015B/1728

9 781662 823244